Book of Elusive Passwords

Kay D Johnson

Johnson, Kay D
Book of Elusive Passwords

ISBN 978-1790479504 (pkb)

**Since this book holds all your
private and valuable information,
please keep this book in a
safe place at all times.**

A

Website:
Email:
User Name:
Password:
Security Question/Hint
Notes:

Website:
Email:
User Name:
Password:
Security Question/Hint
Notes:

Website:
Email:
User Name:
Password:
Security Question/Hint
Notes:

A

Website:
Email:
User Name:
Password:
Security Question/Hint
Notes:

Website:
Email:
User Name:
Password:
Security Question/Hint
Notes:

Website:
Email:
User Name:
Password:
Security Question/Hint
Notes:

A

Website:
Email:
User Name:
Password:
Security Question/Hint
Notes:

Website:
Email:
User Name:
Password:
Security Question/Hint
Notes:

Website:
Email:
User Name:
Password:
Security Question/Hint
Notes:

A

Website:
Email:
User Name:
Password:
Security Question/Hint
Notes:

Website:
Email:
User Name:
Password:
Security Question/Hint
Notes:

User Name:
Password:
Security Question/Hint
Notes:

B

Website:
Email:
User Name:
Password:
Security Question/Hint
Notes:

Website:
Email:
User Name:
Password:
Security Question/Hint
Notes:

Website:
Email:
User Name:
Password:
Security Question/Hint
Notes:

B

Website:
Email:
User Name:
Password:
Security Question/Hint
Notes:

Website:
Email:
User Name:
Password:
Security Question/Hint
Notes:

Website:
Email:
User Name:
Password:
Security Question/Hint
Notes:

B

Website:
Email:
User Name:
Password:
Security Question/Hint
Notes:

Website:
Email:
User Name:
Password:
Security Question/Hint
Notes:

Website:
Email:
User Name:
Password:
Security Question/Hint
Notes:

B

Website:
Email:
User Name:
Password:
Security Question/Hint
Notes:

Website:
Email:
User Name:
Password:
Security Question/Hint
Notes:

Website:
Email:
User Name:
Password:
Security Question/Hint
Notes:

Website:	**C**
Email:	
User Name:	
Password:	
Security Question/Hint	
Notes:	

Website:
Email:
User Name:
Password:
Security Question/Hint
Notes:

Website:
Email:
User Name:
Password:
Security Question/Hint
Notes:

Website:
Email:
User Name:
Password:
Security Question/Hint
Notes:

Website:
Email:
User Name:
Password:
Security Question/Hint
Notes:

Website:
Email:
User Name:
Password:
Security Question/Hint
Notes:

C

Website:
Email:
User Name:
Password:
Security Question/Hint
Notes:

Website:
Email:
User Name:
Password:
Security Question/Hint
Notes:

Website:
Email:
User Name:
Password:
Security Question/Hint
Notes:

C

Website:
Email:
User Name:
Password:
Security Question/Hint
Notes:

Website:
Email:
User Name:
Password:
Security Question/Hint
Notes:

Website:
Email:
User Name:
Password:
Security Question/Hint
Notes:

D

Website:
Email:
User Name:
Password:
Security Question/Hint
Notes:

Website:
Email:
User Name:
Password:
Security Question/Hint
Notes:

Website:
Email:
User Name:
Password:
Security Question/Hint
Notes:

D

| Website: |
| Email: |
| User Name: |
| Password: |
| |
| |
| Security Question/Hint |
| |
| Notes: |
| |

| Website: |
| Email: |
| User Name: |
| Password: |
| |
| |
| Security Question/Hint |
| |
| Notes: |
| |

| Website: |
| Email: |
| User Name: |
| Password: |
| |
| |
| Security Question/Hint |
| |
| Notes: |
| |

D

Website:
Email:
User Name:
Password:
Security Question/Hint
Notes:

Website:
Email:
User Name:
Password:
Security Question/Hint
Notes:

Website:
Email:
User Name:
Password:
Security Question/Hint
Notes:

D

| Website: |
| Email: |
| User Name: |
| Password: |
| |
| |
| Security Question/Hint |
| |
| Notes: |
| |

| Website: |
| Email: |
| User Name: |
| Password: |
| |
| |
| Security Question/Hint |
| |
| Notes: |
| |

| Website: |
| Email: |
| User Name: |
| Password: |
| |
| |
| Security Question/Hint |
| |
| Notes: |
| |

E

Website:
Email:
User Name:
Password:
Security Question/Hint
Notes:

Website:
Email:
User Name:
Password:
Security Question/Hint
Notes:

Website:
Email:
User Name:
Password:
Security Question/Hint
Notes:

Website:
Email:
User Name:
Password:
Security Question/Hint
Notes:

Website:
Email:
User Name:
Password:
Security Question/Hint
Notes:

Website:
Email:
User Name:
Password:
Security Question/Hint
Notes:

E

Website:
Email:
User Name:
Password:
Security Question/Hint
Notes:

Website:
Email:
User Name:
Password:
Security Question/Hint
Notes:

Website:
Email:
User Name:
Password:
Security Question/Hint
Notes:

Website:
Email:
User Name:
Password:
Security Question/Hint
Notes:

Website:
Email:
User Name:
Password:
Security Question/Hint
Notes:

Website:
Email:
User Name:
Password:
Security Question/Hint
Notes:

Website:
Email:
User Name:
Password:
Security Question/Hint
Notes:

Website:
Email:
User Name:
Password:
Security Question/Hint
Notes:

Website:
Email:
User Name:
Password:
Security Question/Hint
Notes:

F

Website:	
Email:	
User Name:	
Password:	
Security Question/Hint	
Notes:	

Website:	
Email:	
User Name:	
Password:	
Security Question/Hint	
Notes:	

Website:	
Email:	
User Name:	
Password:	
Security Question/Hint	
Notes:	

F

Website:
Email:
User Name:
Password:
Security Question/Hint
Notes:

Website:
Email:
User Name:
Password:
Security Question/Hint
Notes:

Website:
Email:
User Name:
Password:
Security Question/Hint
Notes:

Website:	
Email:	
User Name:	
Password:	
Security Question/Hint	
Notes:	

Website:	
Email:	
User Name:	
Password:	
Security Question/Hint	
Notes:	

Website:	
Email:	
User Name:	
Password:	
Security Question/Hint	
Notes:	

G

Website:
Email:
User Name:
Password:
Security Question/Hint
Notes:

Website:
Email:
User Name:
Password:
Security Question/Hint
Notes:

Website:
Email:
User Name:
Password:
Security Question/Hint
Notes:

G

Website:
Email:
User Name:
Password:
Security Question/Hint
Notes:

Website:
Email:
User Name:
Password:
Security Question/Hint
Notes:

Website:
Email:
User Name:
Password:
Security Question/Hint
Notes:

G

Website:
Email:
User Name:
Password:
Security Question/Hint
Notes:

Website:
Email:
User Name:
Password:
Security Question/Hint
Notes:

Website:
Email:
User Name:
Password:
Security Question/Hint
Notes:

G

Website:
Email:
User Name:
Password:
Security Question/Hint
Notes:

Website:
Email:
User Name:
Password:
Security Question/Hint
Notes:

Website:
Email:
User Name:
Password:
Security Question/Hint
Notes:

H

Website:
Email:
User Name:
Password:
Security Question/Hint
Notes:

Website:
Email:
User Name:
Password:
Security Question/Hint
Notes:

Website:
Email:
User Name:
Password:
Security Question/Hint
Notes:

Website:
Email:
User Name:
Password:
Security Question/Hint
Notes:

Website:
Email:
User Name:
Password:
Security Question/Hint
Notes:

Website:
Email:
User Name:
Password:
Security Question/Hint
Notes:

H

Website:
Email:
User Name:
Password:
Security Question/Hint
Notes:

Website:
Email:
User Name:
Password:
Security Question/Hint
Notes:

Website:
Email:
User Name:
Password:
Security Question/Hint
Notes:

Website:
Email:
User Name:
Password:
Security Question/Hint
Notes:

Website:
Email:
User Name:
Password:
Security Question/Hint
Notes:

Website:
Email:
User Name:
Password:
Security Question/Hint
Notes:

I

Website:
Email:
User Name:
Password:
Security Question/Hint
Notes:

Website:
Email:
User Name:
Password:
Security Question/Hint
Notes:

Website:
Email:
User Name:
Password:
Security Question/Hint
Notes:

I

Website:
Email:
User Name:
Password:
Security Question/Hint
Notes:

Website:
Email:
User Name:
Password:
Security Question/Hint
Notes:

Website:
Email:
User Name:
Password:
Security Question/Hint
Notes:

Website:
Email:
User Name:
Password:
Security Question/Hint
Notes:

I

Website:
Email:
User Name:
Password:
Security Question/Hint
Notes:

Website:
Email:
User Name:
Password:
Security Question/Hint
Notes:

I

Website:
Email:
User Name:
Password:
Security Question/Hint
Notes:

Website:
Email:
User Name:
Password:
Security Question/Hint
Notes:

Website:
Email:
User Name:
Password:
Security Question/Hint
Notes:

J

Website:
Email:
User Name:
Password:
Security Question/Hint
Notes:

Website:
Email:
User Name:
Password:
Security Question/Hint
Notes:

Website:
Email:
User Name:
Password:
Security Question/Hint
Notes:

J

Website:
Email:
User Name:
Password:
Security Question/Hint
Notes:

Website:
Email:
User Name:
Password:
Security Question/Hint
Notes:

Website:
Email:
User Name:
Password:
Security Question/Hint
Notes:

J

| Website: |
| Email: |
| User Name: |
| Password: |
| |
| |
| Security Question/Hint |
| |
| Notes: |
| |

| Website: |
| Email: |
| User Name: |
| Password: |
| |
| |
| Security Question/Hint |
| |
| Notes: |
| |

| Website: |
| Email: |
| User Name: |
| Password: |
| |
| |
| Security Question/Hint |
| |
| Notes: |
| |

J

Website:
Email:
User Name:
Password:
Security Question/Hint
Notes:

Website:
Email:
User Name:
Password:
Security Question/Hint
Notes:

Website:
Email:
User Name:
Password:
Security Question/Hint
Notes:

K

Website:
Email:
User Name:
Password:
Security Question/Hint
Notes:

Website:
Email:
User Name:
Password:
Security Question/Hint
Notes:

Website:
Email:
User Name:
Password:
Security Question/Hint
Notes:

K

Website:
Email:
User Name:
Password:
Security Question/Hint
Notes:

Website:
Email:
User Name:
Password:
Security Question/Hint
Notes:

Website:
Email:
User Name:
Password:
Security Question/Hint
Notes:

K

| Website: |
| Email: |
| User Name: |
| Password: |
| |
| |
| Security Question/Hint |
| |
| Notes: |
| |

| Website: |
| Email: |
| User Name: |
| Password: |
| |
| |
| Security Question/Hint |
| |
| Notes: |
| |

| Website: |
| Email: |
| User Name: |
| Password: |
| |
| |
| Security Question/Hint |
| |
| Notes: |
| |

K

Website:
Email:
User Name:
Password:
Security Question/Hint
Notes:

Website:
Email:
User Name:
Password:
Security Question/Hint
Notes:

Website:
Email:
User Name:
Password:
Security Question/Hint
Notes:

L

Website:
Email:
User Name:
Password:
Security Question/Hint
Notes:

Website:
Email:
User Name:
Password:
Security Question/Hint
Notes:

Website:
Email:
User Name:
Password:
Security Question/Hint
Notes:

L

Website:
Email:
User Name:
Password:
Security Question/Hint
Notes:

Website:
Email:
User Name:
Password:
Security Question/Hint
Notes:

Website:
Email:
User Name:
Password:
Security Question/Hint
Notes:

L

Website:
Email:
User Name:
Password:
Security Question/Hint
Notes:

Website:
Email:
User Name:
Password:
Security Question/Hint
Notes:

Website:
Email:
User Name:
Password:
Security Question/Hint
Notes:

L

| Website: |
| Email: |
| User Name: |
| Password: |
| |
| |
| Security Question/Hint |
| |
| Notes: |
| |

| Website: |
| Email: |
| User Name: |
| Password: |
| |
| |
| Security Question/Hint |
| |
| Notes: |
| |

| Website: |
| Email: |
| User Name: |
| Password: |
| |
| |
| Security Question/Hint |
| |
| Notes: |
| |

Website:	**M**
Email:	
User Name:	
Password:	
Security Question/Hint	
Notes:	

Website:
Email:
User Name:
Password:
Security Question/Hint
Notes:

Website:
Email:
User Name:
Password:
Security Question/Hint
Notes:

Website:	
Email:	
User Name:	
Password:	
Security Question/Hint	
Notes:	

Website:	
Email:	
User Name:	
Password:	
Security Question/Hint	
Notes:	

Website:	
Email:	
User Name:	
Password:	
Security Question/Hint	
Notes:	

Website:	**M**
Email:	
User Name:	
Password:	
Security Question/Hint	
Notes:	

Website:
Email:
User Name:
Password:
Security Question/Hint
Notes:

Website:
Email:
User Name:
Password:
Security Question/Hint
Notes:

Website:
Email:
User Name:
Password:
Security Question/Hint
Notes:

Website:
Email:
User Name:
Password:
Security Question/Hint
Notes:

Website:
Email:
User Name:
Password:
Security Question/Hint
Notes:

| Website: |
| Email: |
| User Name: |
| Password: |
| |
| |
| Security Question/Hint |
| |
| Notes: |
| |

| Website: |
| Email: |
| User Name: |
| Password: |
| |
| |
| Security Question/Hint |
| |
| Notes: |
| |

| Website: |
| Email: |
| User Name: |
| Password: |
| |
| |
| Security Question/Hint |
| |
| Notes: |
| |

N

| Website: |
| Email: |
| User Name: |
| Password: |
| |
| |
| Security Question/Hint |
| |
| Notes: |
| |

| Website: |
| Email: |
| User Name: |
| Password: |
| |
| |
| Security Question/Hint |
| |
| Notes: |
| |

| Website: |
| Email: |
| User Name: |
| Password: |
| |
| |
| Security Question/Hint |
| |
| Notes: |
| |

N

Website:
Email:
User Name:
Password:
Security Question/Hint
Notes:

Website:
Email:
User Name:
Password:
Security Question/Hint
Notes:

Website:
Email:
User Name:
Password:
Security Question/Hint
Notes:

N

Website:
Email:
User Name:
Password:
Security Question/Hint
Notes:

Website:
Email:
User Name:
Password:
Security Question/Hint
Notes:

Website:
Email:
User Name:
Password:
Security Question/Hint
Notes:

O

| Website: |
| Email: |
| User Name: |
| Password: |
| |
| |
| Security Question/Hint |
| |
| Notes: |
| |

| Website: |
| Email: |
| User Name: |
| Password: |
| |
| |
| Security Question/Hint |
| |
| Notes: |
| |

| Website: |
| Email: |
| User Name: |
| Password: |
| |
| |
| Security Question/Hint |
| |
| Notes: |
| |

Website:
Email:
User Name:
Password:
Security Question/Hint
Notes:

Website:
Email:
User Name:
Password:
Security Question/Hint
Notes:

Website:
Email:
User Name:
Password:
Security Question/Hint
Notes:

Website:	
Email:	**O**
User Name:	
Password:	
Security Question/Hint	
Notes:	

Website:
Email:
User Name:
Password:
Security Question/Hint
Notes:

Website:
Email:
User Name:
Password:
Security Question/Hint
Notes:

O

Website:
Email:
User Name:
Password:
Security Question/Hint
Notes:

Website:
Email:
User Name:
Password:
Security Question/Hint
Notes:

Website:
Email:
User Name:
Password:
Security Question/Hint
Notes:

P

Website:
Email:
User Name:
Password:
Security Question/Hint
Notes:

Website:
Email:
User Name:
Password:
Security Question/Hint
Notes:

Website:
Email:
User Name:
Password:
Security Question/Hint
Notes:

Website:	
Email:	
User Name:	
Password:	
Security Question/Hint	
Notes:	

Website:	
Email:	
User Name:	
Password:	
Security Question/Hint	
Notes:	

Website:	
Email:	
User Name:	
Password:	
Security Question/Hint	
Notes:	

Website:
Email:
User Name:
Password:
Security Question/Hint
Notes:

Website:
Email:
User Name:
Password:
Security Question/Hint
Notes:

Website:
Email:
User Name:
Password:
Security Question/Hint
Notes:

P

Website:
Email:
User Name:
Password:
Security Question/Hint
Notes:

Website:
Email:
User Name:
Password:
Security Question/Hint
Notes:

Website:
Email:
User Name:
Password:
Security Question/Hint
Notes:

Q

Website:
Email:
User Name:
Password:
Security Question/Hint
Notes:

Website:
Email:
User Name:
Password:
Security Question/Hint
Notes:

Website:
Email:
User Name:
Password:
Security Question/Hint
Notes:

Website:
Email:
User Name:
Password:
Security Question/Hint
Notes:

Website:
Email:
User Name:
Password:
Security Question/Hint
Notes:

Website:
Email:
User Name:
Password:
Security Question/Hint
Notes:

Website:	
Email:	**Q**
User Name:	
Password:	
Security Question/Hint	
Notes:	

Website:
Email:
User Name:
Password:
Security Question/Hint
Notes:

Website:
Email:
User Name:
Password:
Security Question/Hint
Notes:

| Website: |
| Email: |
| User Name: |
| Password: |
| |
| |
| Security Question/Hint |
| |
| Notes: |
| |

| Website: |
| Email: |
| User Name: |
| Password: |
| |
| |
| Security Question/Hint |
| |
| Notes: |
| |

| Website: |
| Email: |
| User Name: |
| Password: |
| |
| |
| Security Question/Hint |
| |
| Notes: |
| |

Website:	**R**
Email:	
User Name:	
Password:	
Security Question/Hint	
Notes:	

Website:
Email:
User Name:
Password:
Security Question/Hint
Notes:

Website:
Email:
User Name:
Password:
Security Question/Hint
Notes:

Website:
Email:
User Name:
Password:
Security Question/Hint
Notes:

Website:
Email:
User Name:
Password:
Security Question/Hint
Notes:

Website:
Email:
User Name:
Password:
Security Question/Hint
Notes:

Website:	
Email:	**R**
User Name:	
Password:	
Security Question/Hint	
Notes:	

Website:
Email:
User Name:
Password:
Security Question/Hint
Notes:

Website:
Email:
User Name:
Password:
Security Question/Hint
Notes:

| Website: |
| Email: |
| User Name: |
| Password: |
| |
| |
| Security Question/Hint |
| |
| Notes: |
| |

| Website: |
| Email: |
| User Name: |
| Password: |
| |
| |
| Security Question/Hint |
| |
| Notes: |
| |

| Website: |
| Email: |
| User Name: |
| Password: |
| |
| |
| Security Question/Hint |
| |
| Notes: |
| |

Website:
Email:
User Name:
Password:
Security Question/Hint
Notes:

S

Website:
Email:
User Name:
Password:
Security Question/Hint
Notes:

Website:
Email:
User Name:
Password:
Security Question/Hint
Notes:

S

Website:
Email:
User Name:
Password:
Security Question/Hint
Notes:

Website:
Email:
User Name:
Password:
Security Question/Hint
Notes:

Website:
Email:
User Name:
Password:
Security Question/Hint
Notes:

S

Website:
Email:
User Name:
Password:
Security Question/Hint
Notes:

Website:
Email:
User Name:
Password:
Security Question/Hint
Notes:

Website:
Email:
User Name:
Password:
Security Question/Hint
Notes:

Website:
Email:
User Name:
Password:
Security Question/Hint
Notes:

Website:
Email:
User Name:
Password:
Security Question/Hint
Notes:

Website:
Email:
User Name:
Password:
Security Question/Hint
Notes:

Website:	**T**
Email:	
User Name:	
Password:	
Security Question/Hint	
Notes:	

Website:
Email:
User Name:
Password:
Security Question/Hint
Notes:

Website:
Email:
User Name:
Password:
Security Question/Hint
Notes:

T

Website:
Email:
User Name:
Password:
Security Question/Hint
Notes:

Website:
Email:
User Name:
Password:
Security Question/Hint
Notes:

Website:
Email:
User Name:
Password:
Security Question/Hint
Notes:

Website:
Email:
User Name:
Password:
Security Question/Hint
Notes:

T

Website:
Email:
User Name:
Password:
Security Question/Hint
Notes:

Website:
Email:
User Name:
Password:
Security Question/Hint
Notes:

T

Website:	
Email:	
User Name:	
Password:	
Security Question/Hint	
Notes:	

Website:	
Email:	
User Name:	
Password:	
Security Question/Hint	
Notes:	

Website:	
Email:	
User Name:	
Password:	
Security Question/Hint	
Notes:	

U

Website:
Email:
User Name:
Password:
Security Question/Hint
Notes:

Website:
Email:
User Name:
Password:
Security Question/Hint
Notes:

Website:
Email:
User Name:
Password:
Security Question/Hint
Notes:

U

Website:
Email:
User Name:
Password:
Security Question/Hint
Notes:

Website:
Email:
User Name:
Password:
Security Question/Hint
Notes:

Website:
Email:
User Name:
Password:
Security Question/Hint
Notes:

Website:	**U**
Email:	
User Name:	
Password:	
Security Question/Hint	
Notes:	

Website:
Email:
User Name:
Password:
Security Question/Hint
Notes:

Website:
Email:
User Name:
Password:
Security Question/Hint
Notes:

U

| Website: |
| Email: |
| User Name: |
| Password: |
| |
| |
| Security Question/Hint |
| |
| Notes: |
| |

| Website: |
| Email: |
| User Name: |
| Password: |
| |
| |
| Security Question/Hint |
| |
| Notes: |
| |

| Website: |
| Email: |
| User Name: |
| Password: |
| |
| |
| Security Question/Hint |
| |
| Notes: |
| |

V

Website:
Email:
User Name:
Password:
Security Question/Hint
Notes:

Website:
Email:
User Name:
Password:
Security Question/Hint
Notes:

Website:
Email:
User Name:
Password:
Security Question/Hint
Notes:

V

Website:
Email:
User Name:
Password:
Security Question/Hint
Notes:

Website:
Email:
User Name:
Password:
Security Question/Hint
Notes:

Website:
Email:
User Name:
Password:
Security Question/Hint
Notes:

V

Website:

Email:

User Name:

Password:

Security Question/Hint

Notes:

Website:

Email:

User Name:

Password:

Security Question/Hint

Notes:

Website:

Email:

User Name:

Password:

Security Question/Hint

Notes:

V

Website:
Email:
User Name:
Password:
Security Question/Hint
Notes:

Website:
Email:
User Name:
Password:
Security Question/Hint
Notes:

Website:
Email:
User Name:
Password:
Security Question/Hint
Notes:

Website:	**W**
Email:	
User Name:	
Password:	
Security Question/Hint	
Notes:	

Website:
Email:
User Name:
Password:
Security Question/Hint
Notes:

Website:
Email:
User Name:
Password:
Security Question/Hint
Notes:

Website:
Email:
User Name:
Password:
Security Question/Hint
Notes:

Website:
Email:
User Name:
Password:
Security Question/Hint
Notes:

Website:
Email:
User Name:
Password:
Security Question/Hint
Notes:

Website:	
Email:	
User Name:	
Password:	
Security Question/Hint	
Notes:	

W

Website:	
Email:	
User Name:	
Password:	
Security Question/Hint	
Notes:	

Website:	
Email:	
User Name:	
Password:	
Security Question/Hint	
Notes:	

Website:
Email:
User Name:
Password:
Security Question/Hint
Notes:

Website:
Email:
User Name:
Password:
Security Question/Hint
Notes:

Website:
Email:
User Name:
Password:
Security Question/Hint
Notes:

Website:	**X**
Email:	
User Name:	
Password:	
Security Question/Hint	
Notes:	

Website:
Email:
User Name:
Password:
Security Question/Hint
Notes:

Website:
Email:
User Name:
Password:
Security Question/Hint
Notes:

Website:
Email:
User Name:
Password:
Security Question/Hint
Notes:

Website:
Email:
User Name:
Password:
Security Question/Hint
Notes:

Website:
Email:
User Name:
Password:
Security Question/Hint
Notes:

X

| Website: |
| Email: |
| User Name: |
| Password: |
| |
| |
| Security Question/Hint |
| |
| Notes: |
| |

| Website: |
| Email: |
| User Name: |
| Password: |
| |
| |
| Security Question/Hint |
| |
| Notes: |
| |

| Website: |
| Email: |
| User Name: |
| Password: |
| |
| |
| Security Question/Hint |
| |
| Notes: |
| |

X

| Website: |
| Email: |
| User Name: |
| Password: |
| |
| |
| Security Question/Hint |
| |
| Notes: |
| |

| Website: |
| Email: |
| User Name: |
| Password: |
| |
| |
| Security Question/Hint |
| |
| Notes: |
| |

| Website: |
| Email: |
| User Name: |
| Password: |
| |
| |
| Security Question/Hint |
| |
| Notes: |
| |

Y

Website:
Email:
User Name:
Password:
Security Question/Hint
Notes:

Website:
Email:
User Name:
Password:
Security Question/Hint
Notes:

Website:
Email:
User Name:
Password:
Security Question/Hint
Notes:

Y

Website:
Email:
User Name:
Password:
Security Question/Hint
Notes:

Website:
Email:
User Name:
Password:
Security Question/Hint
Notes:

Website:
Email:
User Name:
Password:
Security Question/Hint
Notes:

Y

Website:
Email:
User Name:
Password:
Security Question/Hint
Notes:

Website:
Email:
User Name:
Password:
Security Question/Hint
Notes:

Website:
Email:
User Name:
Password:
Security Question/Hint
Notes:

Y

Website:	
Email:	
User Name:	
Password:	
Security Question/Hint	
Notes:	

Website:	
Email:	
User Name:	
Password:	
Security Question/Hint	
Notes:	

Website:	
Email:	
User Name:	
Password:	
Security Question/Hint	
Notes:	

Website:
Email:
User Name:
Password:
Security Question/Hint
Notes:

Website:
Email:
User Name:
Password:
Security Question/Hint
Notes:

Website:
Email:
User Name:
Password:
Security Question/Hint
Notes:

Website:	
Email:	
User Name:	
Password:	
Security Question/Hint	
Notes:	

Website:	
Email:	
User Name:	
Password:	
Security Question/Hint	
Notes:	

Website:	
Email:	
User Name:	
Password:	
Security Question/Hint	
Notes:	

Website:
Email:
User Name:
Password:
Security Question/Hint
Notes:

Website:
Email:
User Name:
Password:
Security Question/Hint
Notes:

Website:
Email:
User Name:
Password:
Security Question/Hint
Notes:

Website:
Email:
User Name:
Password:
Security Question/Hint
Notes:

Website:
Email:
User Name:
Password:
Security Question/Hint
Notes:

Website:
Email:
User Name:
Password:
Security Question/Hint
Notes:

≪ NOTES ≫

≪ NOTES ≫

_____
_____
_____
_____
_____
_____
_____
_____
_____
_____
_____
_____
_____
_____
_____
_____
_____
_____
_____
_____
_____
_____
_____
_____
_____

Enjoying this Book?
Please leave a Review!
I would love to hear your feedback
THANK YOU for purchasing my product.
Your support is greatly appreciated!